James Monroe

By United Library

https://campsite.bio/unitedlibrary

Table of Contents

Disclaimer

This biography book is a work of nonfiction based on the public life of a famous person. The author has used publicly available information to create this work. While the author has thoroughly researched the subject and attempted to depict it accurately, it is not meant to be an exhaustive study of the subject. The views expressed in this book are those of the author alone and do not necessarily reflect those of any organization associated with the subject. This book should not be taken as an endorsement, legal advice, or any other form of professional advice. This book was written for entertainment purposes only.

Introduction

Delve into the life and political career of James Monroe, the fifth president of the United States, in this captivating biography that offers fresh insights into one of America's Founding Fathers. In James Monroe;s book, readers will discover the fascinating journey of a statesman who played a pivotal role in shaping the nation during a crucial era in its history.

Born in 1758, Monroe's life unfolded against the backdrop of the American Revolutionary War, where he served with distinction in the Continental Army. His education under the mentorship of Thomas Jefferson and his early involvement in politics paved the way for a remarkable career that spanned various roles, including governor of Virginia, U.S. senator, and ambassador to both France and Britain.

As a member of the Democratic-Republican Party, Monroe rose to prominence, championing the party's principles and earning a place in Thomas Jefferson's inner circle. His contributions to American diplomacy and foreign affairs were significant, with his name forever associated with the Monroe Doctrine, a bold policy statement that limited European colonialism in the Americas.

Monroe's presidency, known as the Era of Good Feelings, marked the end of the First Party System and a period of relative political harmony. His leadership during the War of 1812 and his involvement in the negotiations for the Louisiana Purchase shaped the nation's territorial expansion. Moreover, his support for the Missouri Compromise and the abolitionist movement left an indelible mark on the nation's path toward resolving complex issues of slavery and westward expansion.

This engaging biography provides a detailed examination of Monroe's political achievements, including his role in shaping American foreign policy and securing the nation's borders. Whether you are a history enthusiast or simply curious about the life of this influential president, this book offers a comprehensive and insightful exploration of a Founding Father's enduring legacy.

James Monroe

James Monroe (b. April 28, 1758 at Monroe Hall in Westmoreland County, Virginia Colony; † July 4, 1831 in New York) was an American politician and the fifth President of the United States from 1817 to 1825.

During the American War of Independence, after dropping out of the College of William & Mary, he served as an officer in the Continental Army. He then began his political career, which took him through the Virginia House of Delegates to the Confederate Congress. At this time he was admitted to the bar and befriended Thomas Jefferson and James Madison, with whom he later became instrumental in determining the policies of the Democratic-Republican Party as the Virginia dynasty. After attending the Virginia ratifying convention and serving several terms in the United States Senate, he was appointed ambassador to France by George Washington in 1794. Although a staunch supporter of the French Revolution, he failed to allay the First Republic's fears of British-American rapprochement after the Jay Treaty. After his recall, which led to a rupture with President Washington, he became governor of Virginia beginning in 1799. In 1803, President Jefferson sent Monroe on a multi-year diplomatic mission to Europe, where he was able to negotiate the Louisiana Purchase, while his stays in London and Madrid were disappointing. He ran unsuccessfully against Madison in the 1808 presidential election. After some time in political obscurity, he was appointed to Madison's cabinet as secretary of state in the spring of 1811 and, during the British-American War, additionally assumed the office of secretary of war for phases.

In 1816, Monroe was the last of the generation of Founding Fathers to be elected American president. One focus of his presidency, in close coordination with Secretary of State John Quincy Adams, was to resolve border disputes with Great Britain, Spain, and the Russian Empire. Despite Andrew Jackson's invasion of the Spanish colony of Florida, the Adams-Onís Treaty was signed in 1819, in which Madrid ceded western and eastern Florida to America. Another central concern of Monroe's was to strengthen the armed forces and coastal fortifications, which he succeeded in doing, particularly for the United States Navy. The defining issue of his tenure was the South American wars of independence, and he, like his entire cabinet, sympathized with the anti-colonial freedom movement. After ratification of the Adams-Onís Treaty, Monroe abandoned benevolent neutrality toward the fledgling republics in Latin America and recognized them diplomatically. On December 2, 1823, he publicly declared with the Monroe Doctrine to regard further colonial endeavors by European powers in the Western

Hemisphere as an unfriendly act. Although never codified, the Monroe Doctrine became the most effective foreign policy declaration by a president in American history. Domestically, Monroe pushed westward expansion and supported the Missouri Compromise, which failed to bridge the division in the United States over the slavery issue but held the American Union together until the War of Secession.

As an elder statesman, he sat on the *Board of Visitors of the* University of Virginia after the presidency ended and chaired the *Virginia Convention in* late 1829. In retirement, Monroe was pressed by considerable financial worries, not least because his expenses as ambassador were not reimbursed to him by Congress until shortly before his death. Previously, he had been forced to sell his remaining land holdings because of a shortage of money. He died impoverished and in the care of his younger daughter on Independence Day 1831 in New York City.

Life

Family and education

James Monroe was born at Monroe Hall in the Virginia Colony, the son of Spence Monroe (1727-1774), a carpenter, and his wife Elizabeth Jones (1730-1772). He had one sister and was the oldest of four brothers. Monroe's father was a patriot and involved in protests against the Stamp Act. Since his land holdings of 200 acres could hardly stand up to competition from the large plantations worked by slaves, he worked as a craftsman and builder, placing him at the lower end of the Gentry. Spence Monroe's great-grandfather was from Scotland and had fled as a royalist to the Anglican colony of Virginia after the defeat of Charles I in the English Civil War. Her mother was the daughter of a Welsh immigrant whose family was one of the wealthiest in King George County. She inherited considerable property with her brother, Joseph Jones. Jones was a judge and one of the most influential members of the House of Burgesses and later a delegate to the Continental Congress. Jones was a friend of George Washington and a close acquaintance of Thomas Jefferson and James Madison.

As was the custom in the Thirteen Colonies at the time, Monroe's parents taught him to read and write. At the age of eleven, his father sent him to the only school in the county, Campbelltown Academy. This was considered the best in the Virginia colony, which is why Monroe was later able to immediately take advanced courses in Latin and mathematics at the College of William & Mary. Like his classmates, he attended the Academy only twelve weeks a year, spending the rest of the time helping on his father's farm. At school he became friends with John Marshall, who later became secretary of state and chief federal judge. In 1772, Monroe's mother died after giving birth to her youngest child, and soon after his father died, leaving him as the eldest son in charge of the family and out of school. Monroe's wealthy Uncle Jones now took care of them and paid off his brother-in-law's debts. He took over Monroe's patronage, shaped his political education, and enrolled him at the College of William & Mary in Williamsburg, where he began his studies in June 1774.

Nearly all of Monroe's fellow students came from wealthy tobacco planter families who formed the ruling class of the Virginia colony and stood to lose the most if taxed by the Kingdom of Great Britain. At this stage of the American Revolution, the mother country took harsh measures against the Thirteen Colonies in response to the Boston Tea Party. In Williamsburg, British Governor John Murray, 4th Earl of Dunmore, dissolved the Assembly after protests from the delegates, whereupon they decided to send a delegation to the First Continental Congress in Philadelphia. When the governor sought to take advantage of the absence of the Burgesses, who had been diverted to Richmond, and had soldiers of the Royal Navy seize the Virginian militia's arms, alarmed militiamen and students of the College of William & Mary, including Monroe, gathered. They marched under arms to the Governor's Palace and demanded that Dunmore return the confiscated gunpowder. When more militiamen, led by Patrick Henry, arrived in Williamsburg, Dunmore agreed to pay compensation for the confiscated goods. Monroe and his fellow students were so incensed by the governor's actions that they conducted daily military drills on campus thereafter. Soon after the battles of Lexington and Concord, which marked the beginning of the American War of Independence, Dunmore fled the city in June 1775 aboard a Royal Navy frigate. On June 24, Monroe and 24 militiamen stormed the Governor's Palace and captured several hundred muskets and swords there.

In the American War of Independence

On January 1, 1776, British marines led by Dunmore stormed Norfolk and burned the town to the ground. When Monroe learned of this, despite mourning the death of his brother Spence, who had died shortly before, he enlisted as a volunteer in the Virginia Infantry along with Marshall and fellow student and close friend John F.

Mercer. Because of his educational background, Monroe was commissioned at the officer rank. He entered the service as a second lieutenant in the 3rd Virginia Regiment, commanded shortly thereafter by Colonel George Weedon. After basic military training at Williamsburg, the regiment marched northward on August 16, 1776, barely six weeks after the American Declaration of Independence, to join the Continental Army under George Washington in Manhattan on September 12. Here Monroe gained his first battlefield experience at the Battle of Harlem Heights. Less than six weeks later, Monroe's regiment was able to repel an enemy raid at night two days before the Battle of White Plains, inflicting a loss of 56 men on the enemy without suffering a casualty. In the Continental Army's retreat on 7 December across the Delaware River in response to the loss of Fort Washington, Monroe's regiment played a central role. On December 26, it was among the first to cross the Delaware under the command of Captain William Washington and opened the Battle of Trenton. At Trenton, Monroe suffered a severe wound to the shoulder, damaging the artery, and survived only thanks to proper first aid by physician John Riker, who had joined Monroe's company only a few hours earlier. That same day, Monroe was promoted to captain by George Washington for his bravery.

After a two-month recovery, Monroe returned to Virginia to recruit troops for the Continental Army under his command. Unsuccessful in this regard, he rejoined the Continental Army in August 1777 and was assigned to General William Alexander, Lord Stirling, as an auxiliary officer. At the Battle of Brandywine on September 11, 1777, he tended the wounded Marie-Joseph Motier, Marquis de La Fayette, with whom he henceforth became close friends. The following month he took part in the Battle of Germantown. By November 20, 1777, he had been promoted to major and served as Lord Stirling's aide-de-camp. During the Battle of Monmouth on June 28, 1778, he was appointed Lord Stirling's aide-de-camp general and helped repel a British attack on his division. Monroe continued to serve until the fall and, probably for financial reasons, returned to Virginia in the spring of 1779. There, the Virginia General Assembly gave him the rank of lieutenant colonel without providing him with sufficient budgetary resources to raise a regiment of his own. Instead, he was assigned as an auxiliary officer to Virginia Governor Thomas Jefferson and, on Jefferson's advice, began studying law at the College of William & Mary. Jefferson, with whom Monroe soon formed a close and lifelong friendship, advised his protégé to pursue a political career and made his library available to him, with the works of Epictetus in particular having a great influence on Monroe. In June 1780, Jefferson, who had been his lifelong mentor since that time, appointed him a military commissioner with the task of maintaining liaison with the Southern Continental Army, which was under the command of General Johann von Kalb in South Carolina. In late 1780 the British moved into Virginia and Monroe, who by then was a colonel, was given command of a regiment for the first time without being able to contribute decisively to the defense. He was denied further command assignments despite extensive efforts. After the Battle of Yorktown, Monroe retired from active duty in November 1781.

BIRTHPLACE OF
JAMES MONROE
APRIL 28, 1758
JULY 4, 1831
FIFTH PRESIDENT OF THE
UNITED STATES
1817 - 1825
GOVERNOR OF VIRGINIA
1799 AND 1811
PROCLAIMED THE MONROE DOCTRINE
DECEMBER 2, 1823
DECLARES THE AMERICAS
NO LONGER SUBJECT TO
EUROPEAN COLONIZATION

MEMORIAL PRESENTED BY
THE NORTHERN NECK LADIES AUXILIARY
TO VETERANS OF FOREIGN WARS
POST 4522, WARSAW
OTHER CONTRIBUTORS:
NORTHERN NECK V.F.W. POST 7167
WILLIAM R. COOPER MEMORIAL
V.F.W. POST 10574
AND
LADIES AUXILIARY TO V.F.W. POST 10574,
COLONIAL BEACH

Early political stations

In 1782, Monroe was elected to the Virginia House of Delegates for King George County. Shortly thereafter, at an unusually young age, he successfully ran for the eight-member Governor's Council. Election to the Fourth Confederate Congress followed in June 1783. He was able to defend this seat in the next two elections. In the Confederate Congress, he distinguished himself at the forefront of those delegates who took a national perspective and did not consider themselves merely citizens of their respective states. Monroe developed a keen interest in American foreign policy and, with a military eye, recognized the basic problem of the United States that later defined his presidency: the conflicts that arose when the young nation's natural expansion collided with the territorial claims of European powers in North America.

He assisted Washington and the Society of the Cincinnati in their scheme to compensate less fortunate veterans of the War for Independence with frontier lands. In this connection, he toured the Ohio Country and later Kentucky in 1784 and 1785. The issue of shifting the frontier westward, which he saw as existential to the future of the United States, preoccupied Monroe throughout his political career. He worked to clarify the legal status of the territories that had been ceded to America for use in the Peace of Paris. Another of Monroe's goals in the Confederate Congress was free navigation on the Mississippi River. His interest in the economic development of the American West, in which Jefferson encouraged him, was also personal, since he, like other Founding Fathers, had been involved in land speculation and had received land grants of 2,000 acres in Kentucky for his service in the Continental Army. Unlike Madison and Washington, who wanted to incorporate these territories into existing states, Monroe and Jefferson favored their inclusion as new states in the United States. Possibly more than any other political leader of his generation, he recognized that the national drive for westward expansion, borne first by settlers and later by European immigrants, could no longer be contained.

On this issue, he came into conflict with Secretary of State John Jay. Jay came from New York City and represented the interests of New England, which was interested in good trade relations with the kingdoms of France and Great Britain, which were potentially threatened by the territorial claims of Virginia and North Carolina west of the Mississippi and in the later Northwest Territory. Moreover, Jay saw westward expansion and the development of waterways there, particularly concerning the port of New Orleans, as serious economic competition for New England's West Indies trade. In 1787, Monroe pushed through the Northwest Ordinance in the Confederate Congress, which was the legal basis for the creation of the Northwest Territory. From this time until the 1810s, Monroe was perceived by the public as the only politician of national importance who championed the interests of the western frontier. While in the Confederate Congress, through Jefferson's mediation, he began a friendship with James Madison.

Monroe's private life during this phase of his life was dominated by two recurring themes: health limitations that regularly confined him to bed, and a shortage of money. He had moved directly into politics after serving in the Continental Army and was still not licensed to practice law, so he lacked an important source of income. On February 16, 1786, he married Elizabeth Kortright, who came from New York City's fine society and belonged to the Episcopal Church, at Trinity Church in Manhattan. They had met when the Confederate Congress was meeting at Federal Hall in Manhattan. Monroe's father-in-law was a formerly wealthy West Indian planter who had been impoverished by the American Revolution. The bond between Monroe and his wife was very close and they were perceived as a well-complementing couple. Later, as First Lady, she made a charming impression on guests due to her grace and natural beauty; however, weak health significantly limited her White House parties compared to her predecessor, Dolley Madison. The marriage produced three children, of whom daughters Eliza (1787-1835) and Maria (1803-1850) reached adulthood. Although Monroe was raised in the Anglican faith, the children were educated according to the teachings of the Episcopal Church.

In the fall of 1786, the Monroes moved to the home of his Uncle Jones in Fredericksburg, where he successfully passed the bar exam. Monroe remained faithful to politics and was soon elected to the Fredericksburg City Council and soon after to the Virginia House of Delegates. In June 1788, he was a participant in the Virginia ratifying convention that voted to adopt the United States Constitution. Monroe took a neutral position between the camps of supporters around Madison and opponents of the Constitution. He called for including in the Constitution guarantees regarding free navigation on the Mississippi River and giving the federal government direct control over the militia in case of defense. In this way, he sought to prevent the creation of a standing army, which proved to be a critical point of contention between the Federalists and the Anti-Federalists, who, as the nucleus of the Democratic-Republican Party, opposed too strong a central government. Monroe also opposed the Electoral College, which he viewed as too corruptible and vulnerable to state interests, and favored direct election of the president. In the end, Monroe voted with the Anti-

Federalists against ratification of the U.S. Constitution, possibly driven by concern that the future federal government would sacrifice the interests of the West to those of the East Coast states. One concession to the Anti-Federalists, who lost by a vote of 79-89 on June 27, 1788, was to recommend to Congress the inclusion of 20 amendments to the Constitution, two of which were Monroe's. In the subsequent election to the 1st Congress of the United States, the Anti-Federalist persuaded Henry Monroe to run against Madison. Madison eventually won the House seat, which did not diminish their friendship.

After this defeat, Monroe moved his family from Fredericksburg to Albemarle County, first to Charlottesville and later to the immediate neighborhood of Monticello, where he purchased an estate and named it *Highland*. Some historians see this change of residence to Virginia's wooded interior as a symbolic break with the planter elite of the East, who cultivated a European lifestyle, and a turn toward the settlers at the foot of the Allegheny Mountains.

In December 1790, Monroe was elected to the U.S. Senate for Virginia, which at the time met in Congress Hall in Philadelphia, then the nation's capital. Because the Senate, unlike the House of Representatives, met behind closed doors, the public paid little attention to it and focused on the lower house. Monroe therefore requested in February 1791 that Senate sessions be held in public, but this was initially rejected and not implemented until February 1794. Two factions soon emerged in the federal government, which was largely under the influence of the Federalists around Treasury Secretary Alexander Hamilton: the Anti-Administration Party, or Republicans, and the Pro-Administration Party, or Federalists. The conflict centered primarily on the question of whether the rights of the individual states or those of the nation were paramount, but also manifested itself in foreign policy terms in the dispute over the extent to which revolutionary France should be supported in the First Coalition War. This dispute dominated political events for the next two decades, first breaking out openly in the debate over the establishment of the First Bank of the United States. When the vote was taken, Monroe was one of five senators who voted against the establishment of this central bank. The Anti-Administration Party began to form around Jefferson in the Democratic-Republican Party, with Madison and Monroe as its organizer and militant party soldier as its principal aides. The political atmosphere became visibly polarized: while the Federalists saw their opponents as unruly and provincial primitives, the Republicans around Jefferson regarded the Federalists as monarchists. When Monroe participated in congressional investigations in 1792 that dealt with Hamilton's illegal transactions to James Reynolds, it led to the exposure of the first political sex scandal in the United States: The payments had been hush money to keep Hamilton's affair with Reynolds' wife secret. Hamilton never forgave Monroe for this public humiliation, which almost led to a duel between the two. In response to pamphlets by Hamilton accusing Jefferson of undermining Washington's authority, Madison and Monroe wrote a series of six essays in 1793-94. These sharply worded replications were largely penned by Monroe.

The split between Federalists and Anti-Federalists was caused not only by differing particular interests, but also by divergent philosophies of life, regional cultures and historical experiences. Virginia-led Republicans were influenced by the self-sufficient plantation system, dependent on land ownership and skeptical of cities, concentrated finance, and central government. Intellectually, Southern planters were influenced by the authors of ancient Greece and the Roman Republic. The Federalists, on the other hand, were primarily urban shopkeepers, merchants, and artisans who depended on maritime trade and did banking. As leader of the Republicans in the Senate, Monroe soon became involved in matters of foreign relations. In 1794 he emerged as an opponent of Hamilton's appointment as ambassador to the United Kingdom and a friend of the First French Republic. Since 1791, he had taken sides with the French

Revolution in several essays under the pseudonym
Aratus.

Ambassador to France

Confidently, Monroe wrote to Washington in April 1794
requesting a personal audience to dissuade him from
appointing Hamilton as ambassador to London.
Washington, who had already dropped this plan, did not
dignify him with a response. Nevertheless, in mid-1794 he
appointed Monroe to succeed Governor Morris as
ambassador to France after Madison and Robert R.
Livingston had declined the offer. Monroe took up this
post at a difficult time: France, Great Britain, and Spain
stood as the United States' most important trading
partners in the First Coalition War and all had territorial
interests in North America: the Kingdom of Great Britain
was the northern neighbor with Upper and Lower Canada,
and the First French Republic claimed ownership in the
west of the huge colony of Louisiana, which it had lost to
Spain in the Peace of Paris in 1763, which had also been in
possession of East and West Florida since the Peace of
Paris in 1783. Louisiana and the Floridas in particular
inhibited further U.S. expansion. America's negotiating
position was made considerably more difficult by a lack of
military strength. In addition, the conflict between Paris
and London in America intensified the confrontation
between the Anglophile Federalists and the Francophile

Republicans. While the Federalists in principle aimed only for independence from Great Britain, the Republicans wanted a revolutionary new form of government, which is why they sympathized strongly with the First French Republic.

Monroe was disingenuously informed about the simultaneous diplomatic mission in London of his former adversary and staunch Federalist Jay by Washington and Secretary of State Edmund Randolph, both of whom had a more neutral stance toward revolutionary France and soon distanced themselves from Paris: While they assured him that Jay's mission in Britain was only concerned with compensation issues stemming from the American War of Independence, the latter actually had a much broader negotiating mandate. In addition to the general mandate of securing continued close relations with France, Monroe was to settle two specific issues with Paris: first, claims for compensation for American merchant ships whose British goods Revolutionary France had seized, and second, free navigation on the Mississippi River. Monroe's impassioned and friendly greeting at the induction ceremony before the National Convention was later criticized by Jay and Randolph for its sentimentality. Washington viewed the speech as "not well developed" in terms of venue and in light of American neutrality in the First Coalition War.

Thus instructed by Randolph, Monroe assumed that he should achieve a deepening of U.S.-French relations, although Washington merely wanted to maintain the status quo. He was visibly torn between his role as a representative of the American government and that as a hawkish partisan politician for the Francophile Republicans. Monroe was able to establish good and useful relations in France, especially with Merlin de Thionville, Jean Lambert Tallien, Antoine Claire Thibaudeau, and Jean François Reubell. From the Welfare Committee, he received a promise on November 21, 1794, that Paris would again abide by the terms of the February 1778 U.S.-French treaty of alliance and grant American ships free access to its ports. The Federalists in the domestic government, however, did not attach much importance to this agreement and continued to focus on relations with London.

When the Jay treaty with the Kingdom of Great Britain, concluded in November 1794, became known, Monroe became entangled in a web of international intrigue and rumor in Paris surrounding the secret treaty arrangements. In response to Monroe's inquiries, Jay first assured him that the agreement with London in no way contradicted the existing treaty with France, whereupon Monroe rashly promised the French that he would inform them of the exact terms of the Jay Treaty. Shortly thereafter, Monroe received the text of the treaty with instructions, now exactly to the contrary, not to disclose its contents to France under any circumstances. Although a Paris newspaper published the text of the Jay Treaty in August 1795, Monroe was still under orders to assure France that this agreement did not alter their friendship.

In February 1795, Monroe secured the release of all American citizens imprisoned since the French Revolution and the wife of his friend the Marquis de La Fayette. In July 1794, he had already arranged for the release of Thomas Paine and taken him in. When the latter worked on a diatribe against Washington despite Monroe's objections, they parted ways again in the spring of 1796. Monroe convinced the French to include navigation rights on the Mississippi River in their peace negotiations with Spain, which eventually resulted in the Peace of Basel. Since Monroe had acted as an unofficial mediator for Spain with France, Madrid was willing to make this concession, which was finally fixed in the Treaty of San Lorenzo on October 27, 1795, granting America limited rights to use the port of New Orleans in addition to free navigation on the Mississippi.

Immediately after Timothy Pickering succeeded Secretary of State Randolph, who had been the only Francophile member of Washington's cabinet, in December 1795, he worked to dismiss Monroe. When Monroe reported his replies to the Directory complaining about the Jay Treaty on March 25, 1796, he sent this as a summary and not fully documented because Paris asked for a redraft of this correspondence. Pickering saw this as a sign of Monroe's unsuitability and, together with Hamilton, convinced Washington to replace Monroe as ambassador. Pickering's letter of dismissal, written on July 29, 1796, and deliberately delayed in being sent, did not reach Monroe until November 1796, thus preventing his return before the presidential election. By the time he left, Monroe had yet to see the progress he had made reversed and France resume seizures on American ships as well as end diplomatic relations with America in response to Congress' passage of the Jay Treaty. Monroe's biographer Gary Hart sees this failure as ultimately rooted in his transference of America's polarized domestic political conflict to the much more complex web of European tensions. In this phase, Monroe's aggressive approach to foreign relations and his self-image of an active role for America in world politics that went beyond mere protection, which distinguished him from all the other Founding Fathers, became apparent for the first time.

Governor of Virginia and Louisiana Purchase

After returning from Paris in 1797, Monroe was in New York for some time to seek redress from Pickering for his deposition, which he perceived as unjust. Back home in

Virginia, he published a defense outlining that he and the friendship with France had been sacrificed for the sake of rapprochement with London. This challenged John Adams to a vigorous counterattack. Finally, in 1797, with the support of Jefferson and Madison, Monroe wrote *A view of the conduct of the executive in the foreign affairs of the United States, connected with the mission to the French Republic, during the years 1794, 5, & 6.* which was over 400 pages long and sharply attacked Washington's government, accusing it of acting against America's interests. For Washington, this marked the final break with his former officer and prompted him to publish a scathing critique of Monroe. Monroe was already in considerable debt at this stage, as his pay as ambassador had fallen far short of necessary expenses and his private income was far too low to cover these costs.

In 1799, Monroe was elected governor of Virginia. At this time, the Federalists began to decline, becoming increasingly entangled in camp battles between Hamilton and Adams, especially over the issue of quasi-war with France. On the Republican side, with Jefferson dropping out as vice president to lead the opposition and Madison not wanting to take advantage of the Federalists' plight, Monroe filled the void. He developed initiatives beyond the limited powers of a governor without being able to accomplish much with them. Like his mentor Jefferson, he attached central importance to the public education system in particular. Monroe also campaigned for state support of militia training and equipment. After Gabriel Prosser's plans for a slave revolt were uncovered in late August 1800, Monroe convened the militia, had guns and gunpowder removed from all stores, and secured the prison where the conspirators were imprisoned with stockades. When the general fear, fueled by the slave rebellions of the Haitian Revolution at the time, proved groundless and retaliation failed to materialize after the execution of the conspirators, he disbanded all but a few of the militia by October 18. After three years in office, Monroe retired. Not much later, Jefferson, by then the American president, asked him to go on another diplomatic mission to France. There he was to assist Ambassador Livingston and negotiate with Paris over the rights to use the port of New Orleans, free navigation on the Mississippi River, and the two Floridas. Jefferson saw the first two points as at risk because the Louisiana colony had been ceded by Spain to the First French Republic in the Third Treaty of San Ildefonso in 1800. On January 11, 1803, the president finally appointed Monroe an envoy with special negotiating powers and ambassador to London.

Once in Paris, Monroe intervened in the negotiations for the Louisiana Purchase, which had until then been conducted for America by Ambassador Livingston. Although the latter had negotiated only a cession of New

Orleans to America, Napoleon Bonaparte, through his foreign minister Charles-Maurice de Talleyrand-Périgord, offered the acquisition of the entire colony of Louisiana, while declaring western and eastern Florida to continue to belong to Spain. This contradicted Jefferson's stipulations, which had stated the acquisition of both Floridas and New Orleans as a goal. Nevertheless, the deal was struck and the Louisiana Purchase treaty signed on April 30, 1803. At a dinner the following day, Monroe was introduced to Napoleon. In their conversation, Napoleon predicted a coming war between America and Britain, which he was correct about. Shortly thereafter, Monroe was sent on to London to negotiate the forced recruitment of American sailors for the Royal Navy and a possible defensive alliance to protect their own maritime trade. Monroe stayed in London from July 1803 until the late fall of 1804. Without having made significant progress in the United Kingdom of Great Britain and Ireland, Monroe was ordered on to Spain to negotiate the Floridas. When he arrived in Madrid on January 2, 1803, he found a poisoned atmosphere for talks, which the American ambassador to Spain, Charles Pinckney, had provided with crude threats of violence. In negotiations on the outstanding territorial issues affecting New Orleans, West Florida, and the Rio Grande, Monroe made no headway and was treated condescendingly. Frustrated, he left Spain after six months and returned to

London, where he spent the next year and a half negotiating trade and economic agreements and, most importantly, the British practice of shanghaiing American seamen. In English ports, he was able to see American prize ships enter with his own eyes.

In the political offside

In early 1806, John Randolph of Roanoke asked him to run in two years against Secretary of State Madison, who was being groomed by Jefferson to succeed him. Monroe declined this request for the time being. Meanwhile, working with envoy William Pinkney, he reached an understanding with London that settled a variety of outstanding financial and economic issues. Jefferson rejected this agreement, however, because it left out forced enlistments. Moreover, the president was concerned with maintaining anti-British sentiment in America, from which Madison benefited, although he denied this motive to Monroe. Monroe perceived the rejection of his negotiation outcome as a slight and felt his friendship with Jefferson and Madison deeply shaken, which is why his personal relationship with the two cooled for some time. After returning to America in December 1807, the still incensed Monroe nevertheless decided to run against Madison in the 1808 presidential election, demonstrating the strength of his political position in Virginia. Monroe was the candidate of the so-called "Old Republicans" around Randolph of Roanoke and John Taylor of Caroline, who regarded Jefferson and Madison as traitors to republican ideals because they had expanded the powers of the federal government vis-à-vis the individual states.

After a clear defeat by Madison, in which he failed to win a single vote in the Electoral College, Monroe, disgraced by most Republicans because of the candidacy, retreated into private life for the next few years. This marked the nadir of a difficult period marked by losses and disappointments since the Louisiana Purchase. Plans to sell his second home in Loudon County, Oak Hill, and use the proceeds to renovate and expand Highland fell through because of low real estate prices. He, like his neighbor Jefferson, experimented with novel horticultural techniques to switch from tobacco, the value of which was steadily declining, to wheat. In September 1808, his daughter Eliza married Judge George Hay, who later became one of President Monroe's key political advisors. In 1810 he rehabilitated himself in the party and was elected to the Virginia House of Delegates in April of that year. On January 16, 1811, he again became governor of Virginia, which remained only a brief episode, since less than two months later Albert Gallatin, acting on Madison's behalf, asked him if he would be willing to succeed Robert Smith as secretary of state.

Ministers in the Madison Cabinet and the British-American War

On the promise that he would be needed in Madison's cabinet as an independent minister and not merely as a mouthpiece for the president, Monroe agreed and became secretary of state in March 1811. Monroe's and Madison's cordial association had by now become a complex and professional relationship. For both the president and the secretary of state, who worked closely together and had few differences, the conflict with Great Britain was the dominant issue over the next few years, and to a lesser extent that with France. London's refusal to listen to American complaints, particularly about forced enlistments, drove both countries ever further toward war. Monroe and Madison agreed that the prestige and interest of the United States did not permit such discrimination. According to Ammon, Monroe's entry into the cabinet meant that a resolution of the continuing controversies between America and Britain became inevitable, whether by means of a peaceful understanding or armed conflict. Although as ambassador to London a few years earlier he had negotiated an agreement that Jefferson had rejected, he brought a more bellicose mood to the Cabinet. At the State of the Union Address in November 1811, Madison called for raising an auxiliary force and enlarging the United States Navy. Monroe was given the task of pushing these schemes through Congress. With Henry Clay and Madison, Monroe planned a new embargo against Great Britain, which passed Congress in March 1812 and served as a test run to see if there was a political majority for war. On June 1, 1812, Madison finally declared war, which the Senate approved by a narrow majority two weeks later.

After the outbreak of the British-American War, Monroe sought military command, especially since he attached only secondary importance to the State Department and diplomacy. After the British Army's successful siege of Detroit in August 1812, he wanted to lead the recapture of Detroit and proposed Jefferson as his successor in the State Department, which the president promptly rejected. Instead, Madison made him acting secretary of war in January 1813, succeeding the unsuccessful William Eustis. Monroe turned over the acting head of the State Department to Richard Rush. Monroe quickly prepared a detailed report on the military manpower needed for coastal defenses and the planned summer offensive. He envisioned recruiting an additional 20,000 regular soldiers on a one-year basis. Monroe's appointment as official secretary of that department was prevented by the Senate in order not to further increase the dominance of Virginian politicians in key positions. According to Madison's biographer Gary Wills, Monroe, on the advice of his son-in-law Hay, had intended only a short-term stint as secretary of war from the outset, fearing for his prospects of his own presidency in that position in the face of a looming long and unpopular war. Instead, in February 1813, John Armstrong Jr, a bitter rival of Monroe's, became official secretary of war. Suspicious, Monroe spied on Armstrong's ministerial correspondence when he perceived a front-line military command outside the capital. When British warships first appeared in the Potomac River estuary in the summer of that year and Monroe urged that defensive measures be taken for Washington, D.C., and that a military intelligence service be established in the form of a pony express to the Chesapeake Bay, the Secretary of War rejected this as unnecessary. Thus lacking a functioning reconnaissance force, Monroe assembled a small cavalry unit on his own and henceforth scouted the bay himself until the British withdrew from it.

After Napoleon's defeat in the Sixth Coalition War in the summer of 1814, the British focused on the American theater of war and prepared for an invasion of the capital. Rumors of this, which warned Armstrong, were again dismissed by the latter. When a British fleet of 50 warships and 5,000 soldiers massed again at the mouth of the Potomac on August 16, 1814, Madison had seen enough and organized with Monroe to defend the Washingtons. Monroe personally scouted the Chesapeake Bay with a squad and on August 21 sent the president a warning of the impending invasion, allowing Madison and his wife to escape in time to evacuate state property and residents. Three days later, Monroe met the President and Cabinet at the Washington Navy Yard for a desperate attempt to make the defense of the capital possible after all. He then rode on to Bladensburg to support General Tobias Stansbury without being able to prevent defeat at the Battle of Bladensburg. The British then moved into the District of Columbia, sacked the town, and burned the public buildings. Shortly thereafter, Madison accepted Armstrong's resignation and this time appointed Monroe not only acting but permanent Secretary of War. Since General William H. Winder was standing in Baltimore, Monroe, as *Secretary of War, was* also the acting general for Washington during this period.

As Secretary of War, Monroe broke with the Republican doctrine of leaving national defense to state militias and planned to call up a conscript army of 100,000 men to repel the British invasion threatening from Canada. To accomplish this, all men between the ages of 18 and 45 were to be divided into groups of one hundred, with the responsibility of providing four serviceable soldiers each. Due to the imminent end of the war, this was never implemented. In September 1814, Monroe focused on assisting General Samuel Smith in the defense of Baltimore. After winning the Battle of Baltimore, he finally succeeded in throwing the British out of the Chesapeake

Bay. War expenses made it necessary for the president to break with another orthodox Republican belief and establish a new central bank after the charter of the First Bank of the United States expired in 1811. Monroe, who was one of the first party leaders to recognize that the Republicans had changed since 1800 and that their supporters were now more urban and bank-friendly, particularly in New England and the Mid-Atlantic states, did not resist. Moreover, he had taken on further debt to pay for war expenses out of his own pocket. After the favorable Peace of Ghent and Andrew Jackson's victory at the Battle of New Orleans, Monroe resigned as Secretary of War on March 15, 1815, and resumed leadership of the State Department. Monroe, who as Secretary of War claimed victories at New Orleans and at the Battle of Plattsburgh, emerged from the British-American War politically stronger and a promising presidential candidate. Before leaving the War Department, he prepared a report for the Senate Committee on Military Affairs recommending a peacetime regular army of 20,000 men and a reinforcement of the coastal defenses, which represented a doubling from manpower levels before the War of 1812. For the next six months he took care of his health, which had been attacked by the enormous workload in the years before.

Presidential election 1816

He returned to the capital in October 1815 and was tipped to succeed Madison, as the State Department counted as a stepping stone to the presidency. While Monroe never enjoyed Jefferson's great popularity, he was widely respected. As Jefferson did with himself at the time, President Madison acted in an outwardly neutral manner as Monroe prepared his candidacy for the 1816 election. Nevertheless, it was widely believed that Madison supported Monroe as his successor. Since there was no longer a serious opposition party because of the decline of the Federalists, who were perceived as disloyal because of their pro-British stance and opposition to the War of 1812, the Democratic-Republican caucus in Congress was crucial to Monroe's victory. In this he was able to defeat his party's rival, Treasury Secretary William Harris Crawford, by a vote of 65-54. Elected as Monroe's running mate was Daniel D. Tompkins. In the November 1816 presidential election, he won clearly against Federalist Rufus King, winning a 183-34 majority in the Electoral College. Monroe's inauguration as the last president from the generation of the Founding Fathers took place on March 4, 1817.

Presidency

During his inaugural address, Monroe praised the courage of his countrymen in the British-American War and America as a vital and prosperous nation. The largest portion of his speech was devoted to national security. Monroe called for more attention to be paid to the military and for coastal fortifications to be strengthened. He cautioned against viewing the United States' geopolitical insularity as a sufficient protective factor, especially since the nation depends on secure sea lanes and fisheries. In future wars, which could not be ruled out, the adversary could destroy the American Union if it was not strong enough, causing it to lose its character as well as its freedom. Further, foreign policy goals were easier to achieve from a position of strength than from one of weakness. Because Monroe was the first president to take office during a period of peace and economic stability, the term "Era of Good Feelings" was soon coined for it. This period was characterized by the unchallenged dominance of the Republicans, who by the end of Madison's term had adopted some of the Federalists' content, such as the creation of a central bank and protective tariffs. Although this made the partisan political situation considerably less heated and polarized than it had been during the presidential election of 1800, by the end of Monroe's term in particular, Republicans below the level of official policy were characterized by severe fragmentation, fiercely rival factions in states such as New York and Virginia, and bitter personal rivalries. Monroe saw it as the president's duty to rise above these conflicts, which is why he remained passive to this development even as it reached into the governing team. Historian Hermann Wellenreuther sees this as a deficit of Monroe's that contributed to the polarization of the political landscape.

Geographical considerations played an important role for Monroe in creating the Cabinet. He wanted to increase the reach of the Republicans and the unity of the nation by selecting people from different regions of the United States for the important ministerial posts. Of particular importance here was the State Department. Since of the first five presidents all but John Adams were Virginians, so that there was already talk of a Virginia dynasty, Monroe wanted to avoid any suspicion of favoritism toward that state. Not only for these reasons did Monroe appoint John Quincy Adams, the son of the second president, as his secretary of state, but also because the latter's exceptional diplomatic talent was undisputed and because, as a supporter of Jefferson's trade embargo in 1807, he had broken with the Federalists. They had known each other since the peace negotiations with Great Britain in 1814, in which Adams had participated with great intensity. Their personal relationship became the most important to Monroe during his presidency. The achievements of their collaboration in this early phase of the United States were matched only by the working relationship of Jefferson and Madison. Adams provided the president with position papers at their daily working meetings, which the president edited or referred any follow-up questions arising from them back to Adams for clarification. He called the Cabinet together less to seek advice and more to build consensus among the ministers and himself, since his positions were usually settled before the meeting.

Until the completion of the restoration of the White House in September 1817, which had been burned by British troops after the Battle of Bladensburg, Monroe lived in what is now the Cleveland Abbe House. This house had already been his residence as Secretary of State and Secretary of War. Reviving a tradition abandoned after Washington, Monroe toured the country during his presidency, such as in May 1818 when he visited forts on the Chesapeake Bay and around Norfolk. Unlike the first president, this was intended less as a symbolic gesture of unity than as a way to drum up local support for the national defense budget. Specifically, he was concerned with establishing a line of forts on the coast as a line of defense, better securing the northern frontier, and building depots and shipyards for the Navy, as he reiterated in his first State of the Union address on December 2, 1817. This became a focus of his presidency, which he reiterated in the speech delivered at his second inauguration in March 1821. In March 1819, Monroe made another visiting trip that took him through Norfolk to Nashville, where he had a week-long meeting with Jackson. In addition, he visited fortifications and the construction sites of Forts Monroe and Calhoun.

In his final State of the Union address in 1824, Monroe announced a reduction in the national debt and appealed one last time for national defense and protection of maritime trade routes with a chain of coastal fortifications and a strong navy. In this address, he looked not to Europe or South America, as he had so often done before, but, like much of the nation as a whole, to the Wild West. He asked Congress to authorize the construction of a fort at the mouth of the Columbia River and to continue to maintain a naval squadron on the West Coast. In the contentious and intensely fought presidential campaign of 1824 between Republicans Jackson, Adams, Crawford, and Clay, Monroe took no part and refused to name his favorite. By the time he left the White House, the political scene was fragmented to an unprecedented degree and characterized by personal rivalries.

Defense Policy

Upon taking office, Monroe faced several foreign policy and security challenges. In the Pacific Northwest, American territorial claims clashed with those of czarist Russia, while navigation rights on rivers in the West remained in dispute and settlers there encountered resistance from North American Indians. In the south, on the border with the Spanish colony of Florida, unrest was caused by Seminole uprisings, which eventually resulted in the First Seminole War, and piracy, against which a weak Spanish administration did nothing. Last but not least, the United States' attitude toward the Latin American republics that emerged during the South American wars of independence had to be clarified. On the one hand, these border conflicts and protection against interference by foreign powers on the North American continent preoccupied Monroe's administration to a great extent; on the other hand, peace in Europe after the Congress of Vienna offered scope for normalizing relations with the European powers.

While still a senator in Congress, Monroe had blocked attempts by Washington's administration to increase the size of the regular army. As governor of Virginia, he had advocated strengthening the state's militia, but this had been rejected on cost grounds. About this time, his attitude began to change toward a standing army, which had been rejected by classical republicans in ancient times because it could be abused as a means of tyranny in peacetime. The British-American War finally convinced Monroe that the national security of an expanding America could no longer be provided by the militia alone.

The Navy survived the budget cuts resulting from the economic crisis of 1819 better than the United States Army. This was largely because it proved indispensable in protecting American merchant ships against piracy. In his last year in office, Monroe pushed an eight-year fleet-building program through Congress that had a scope of nine ships of the line, twelve frigates, and three floating batteries. Two years earlier, the permanent stationing of United States Navy ships off the American West Coast had been established. At Adams's urging, Monroe sent a frigate to the Antarctic Peninsula to forestall British expeditions and territorial claims there.

As had been the case for his predecessors, maritime trade was an important issue for Monroe. In particular, this involved the condemnation of the maritime slave trade that had been agreed to in the Peace of Ghent. Monroe and Adams stood by this agreement but did not wish to surrender state sovereign rights to an international authority with permission to search American ships. Public opinion, which had first sided with the President, began to turn under pressure from Northeastern abolitionists and the American Colonization Society. This society urged the return of freedmen to Africa, where it had established the colony of Liberia. When congressional committees proved willing to allow international inspections with limited rights, Adams blocked it. Monroe then sought a bilateral agreement with Great Britain that allowed searches on the high seas, despite opposition from his secretary of state. He hoped this agreement would resolve other outstanding issues, including border disputes over Maine and Oregon Country. When Congress limited inspections to African coastal waters, London dropped the negotiations. After that, the door was permanently closed to joint action by America and Britain against the slave trade.

Adams-Onís contract

Several lengthy cabinet meetings were held at the end of October 1817. One item on the agenda was the declarations of independence by some former Spanish colonies in South America and the question of how to react to them. Another was the increasing piracy, especially emanating from Amelia Island. Piracy on the southern border with the Floridas was increased by smugglers, slave traders, and privateers who had fled Spanish colonies over which the mother country had lost control. As usual, Monroe had sent questions and briefings to the ministers beforehand and then engaged in a lengthy discussion with the Cabinet to seek clarification. After three meetings, the decision was reached that same month to use the United States Army against the marauders at Amelia Island and at Galveston. In addition, the Georgia and Alabama border areas with the Floridas, where the Seminoles were rebelling, were to be pacified. General Edmund P. Gaines received authorization to place the Seminoles in the territory of the Spanish colony of Florida should they flee across the border there. Only in the event that they sought refuge in Spanish forts was Gaines to refrain from further pursuit.

In April 1818, the Cabinet decided to leave Gaines's successor, Jackson, who had led operations against piracy in Amelia Island, stationed in the Floridas until Madrid had established a functioning administration there. Jackson's military actions posed a communications problem for Monroe, as situation reports always arrived in Washington with a long delay. Thus, during this cabinet meeting, it was not yet known that Jackson, after eliminating the pirates on his own, had expelled the Spanish governor of West Florida along with his crew from Fort Barrancas in Pensacola, risking war with Spain. Jackson had made this decision after learning that the Seminoles had been aided by this garrison in their raids on Georgia settlements. Regarding the South American wars of independence, ambassadors to Europe were instructed to declare on their own authority that the United States regarded any interference in South American affairs as a hostile act. The Cabinet did not meet again on the new situation in Florida until July 15, 1818, when Monroe returned from a trip from North Carolina.

At this meeting, led by Secretary of War John C. Calhoun, all cabinet members except the Secretary of State condemned Jackson's actions and called for an investigation. Adams endorsed Jackson's operations, saw them covered by his orders, and advocated holding fast to the Pensacola and Saint Marks conquests. Monroe shortly thereafter fixed the official government position in a letter from Adams to Spanish Ambassador Luis de Onís, which he edited accordingly, removing all justification for

Jackson's actions. In addition, Monroe emphasized that Jackson had exceeded his orders but had come to a new assessment of the situation based on previously unknown information at the war site. However, Jackson had told him in a confidential letter six months earlier that East Florida was to be annexed. According to historian Sean Wilentz, Jackson's willingness to conquer Florida at the slightest provocation had almost certainly been the reason for Monroe to entrust him with this mission. Monroe offered Spain to vacate the forts again as soon as they sent appropriate garrisons. According to Ammon, Monroe's position had been firmed before the Cabinet meeting, but he had carried it out anyway in order to position himself between the two factions of opinion among his ministers. In this way, he could, on the one hand, keep under control any movement in Congress aimed at censuring Jackson and, on the other, retain Jackson's conquests as a tactical advantage, especially since the latter had gained the status of a popular hero. By stating that Jackson had transgressed his instructions, Monroe avoided constitutional problems for his government and a declaration of war by Spain and its allies. In a letter to Jackson on July 19, he explained why he had not officially approved the high-handed conquests. The lack of presidential backing led to a lifelong rift between Monroe and Jackson.

Although Jackson continued to capture military posts in the Spanish colony of Florida, Adams managed to negotiate quietly with de Onís for the acquisition of the two Floridas and for the establishment of the western boundary of the Missouri Territory. This was the former Louisiana Territory, which had been renamed to avoid confusion with the newly created state of Louisiana. The Missouri Territory abutted the Viceroyalty of New Spain to the west. At issue was the New Spanish province of Texas, whose annexation American public opinion vehemently demanded. After Adams advanced in negotiations over the Floridas and approached the point of contention of the western border of the Missouri Territory, Monroe skillfully increased pressure on Madrid and announced that he would consult with Jackson on further action on the issue. Ultimately, Adams was able to convince the president to be satisfied with the acquisition of the two Floridas, to forego Texas for the time being, and to accept as the border with the Viceroyalty of New Spain the course of the Sabine, Red, and Arkansas Rivers. Another decisive factor was that the northeastern states viewed the expansion to the south and west skeptically, fearing an expansion of slavery into these regions. In addition, Monroe foresaw a new negotiating partner for the Texas question in the near future in light of the Mexican War of Independence.

On February 22, 1819, the Adams-Onís Treaty was signed. It established the acquisition of the Spanish colony of Florida by the United States and opened the Missouri Territory north of 42° latitude westward to the Pacific Ocean, creating the Oregon Country. Washington thus gained access to the Pacific Ocean for the first time in a form that was binding under international law. The Adams-Onís Treaty was ratified by Congress in 1821. This marked the end of negotiations between Spain and America, which had lasted, with interruptions, for more than 25 years. In the Oregon Country itself, America's economic interests and territorial claims collided with those of Russian America, which had trading posts down to San Francisco Bay, and Great Britain. The situation intensified in the fall of 1821 when Saint Petersburg, north of 51° latitude, closed America's Pacific territorial sea to foreign ships within a 100-mile zone, thus shifting its territorial claim southward by four degrees of latitude. In April 1824, Monroe reached an agreement with Russia that limited Russian America's territorial claims to territories north of 54° 40' latitude.

South American wars of independence

The South American wars of independence were the political issue that most preoccupied Monroe and Adams during their tenure. Monroe had less political control than he would have liked in this matter and was pushed to some extent by Clay beginning in 1821. The latter, as Speaker of the House of Representatives, demanded diplomatic recognition of the United Provinces of the Río de la Plata and capering comprehensive support for anti-colonial liberation movements. Clay wanted to use this commitment to build himself up as Monroe's successor. Public opinion in the United States was overwhelmingly on the side of the South American revolutionaries, a position that Monroe, as a staunch Republican, emotionally shared. His initial stance was to favor the liberation movements as much as possible without risking war with Spain while negotiations with Madrid over the Floridas and the western border of the Missouri Territory were underway. For Monroe and Adams, resolving the border disputes had a higher priority, thus creating the classic case of a conflict between interest politics and value orientation. After their respective declarations of independence, the South American republics quickly sent emissaries to Washington to seek diplomatic recognition and economic and trade relations. Monroe, in turn, sent three plenipotentiaries on a naval vessel to South America to sound out the situation on the ground. Monroe sent word to a representative of the United Provinces of the Río de la Plata through Adams in 1818 that his attitude in the conflict was one of "impartial neutrality," which partially reassured Clay's faction. Although not diplomatically recognized for the time being, the fledgling republics enjoyed almost all the benefits of a sovereign nation in economic, commercial, and diplomatic relations with the United States. Monroe and Adams also assured the later emissaries of other republics of friendly relations.

In all of his State of the Union speeches, Monroe expressed sympathy for the South Americans' struggle for freedom, including in 1820, although Adams had advised against it. After the Adams-Onís Treaty was concluded, pressure on Monroe to show consideration for Madrid in this matter lessened. After Spain and America had fully ratified the Adams-Onís Treaty in February 1821 and a liberal government had come to power in Madrid, Monroe proposed diplomatic recognition of the United Provinces of the Río de la Plata, Mexico, Chile, Peru, and Colombia to the Senate on March 8, 1822. The special significance of the diplomatic recognition of the South American republics lay in two aspects: First, it launched a political discussion on the continuation of colonialism; second, it redefined the basis of relations between the Americas, Europe, and the Western Hemisphere. To a lesser extent, this move led to the question of the extent to which the United States should play an active role in the affairs of Europe.

Indian Policy

Monroe was the first president to visit the American West, and in his cabinet he entrusted Secretary of War Calhoun with departmental responsibility for this region, which included border security and Indian policy. To prevent the relentless attacks on Indian settlement areas that accompanied the steady westward expansion, he advocated dividing the territories between the federal territories and the Rocky Mountains and assigning them to different tribes for settlement. The districts were each to be given a civil government and a school system. In an address to Congress on March 30, 1824, Monroe advocated relocating Indians living in United States territory to lands beyond the western frontier where they could continue their ancestral way of life. Overall, he appealed that humanitarian considerations and benevolence should prevail in dealing with the Indians. Nevertheless, he shared in principle Jackson's and Calhoun's reservations about sovereign Indian nations as an obstacle to further development of the West. Like Washington and Jefferson, he wanted to expose the Indians to the benefits of American culture and Western civilization for their own good, in part to thereby save them from extinction. Thus, Monroe's rhetoric of independent Indian nations, which had been the foundation of American Indian policy until the War of 1812, was mere lip service.

Missouri Compromise

With the founding of the United States, the admission of new states was always linked to the slavery issue. In the period between 1817 and 1819, Mississippi, Alabama and Illinois were recognized as new states. As a result of the rapid expansion, an increased economic gap between the regions and a shift of power in Congress to the disadvantage of the southern states became apparent, which therefore saw their plantation economy, which had been dependent on slavery, increasingly threatened. In addition, resistance to slavery was beginning to form in the northern states at this time. When Missouri applied for admission to the American Union in 1819, the first fierce clash between opponents and supporters of slavery and a division of the entire country into two hostile camps occurred over the question of admission conditions.

The extent to which Monroe lived up to his presidential leadership role in crafting the Missouri Compromise remains controversial today, with the majority of historians emphasizing Monroe's passivity. He viewed the question of admission terms less from a moral than from a political perspective. Unusually, Monroe did not convene a cabinet meeting on the matter, as was usually his style on pressing issues. He probably wanted to avoid a confrontation between Adams, a staunch abolitionist, and cabinet members from the slave states. Privately, Monroe made it known that he would veto any bill that dictated a particular stance on the slavery issue as a condition of admission for Missouri. Secretly, Monroe knew from Virginian politicians in Congress that confidential discussions were taking place there about drawing a compromise line west of Missouri on the 36° 30′ parallel. Future states north of this line were to be slave-free, while those south of it were to be free to decide for themselves. Monroe himself was a slaveholder and, like Jefferson, felt morally torn on the issue. His scruples, however, did not go beyond the conventional view of educated Virginians of the late 18th century that slavery was an evil and should eventually be ended.

After this compromise was introduced in the Senate, Monroe quietly indicated that he would sign any bill based on this agreement. When this became known in his native Virginia, the political establishment there reacted with outrage. In a letter to Jefferson at the beginning of 1820, Monroe described the Missouri question as the most dangerous to the cohesion of the American Union that he had yet encountered. To organize a majority in Congress, Monroe activated Adams and Crawford and Calhoun to use their political influence in the New England and Southern states. On February 26, 1820, the Missouri Compromise finally passed Congress. In March, Monroe had the bills before him that set the compromise line and left Missouri free to make its own decisions about slavery, while Maine was admitted to the Union as a slave-free state to compensate. The Cabinet unanimously agreed that Congress had constitutional legitimacy to ban slavery in territories and future states. Monroe was warned by friends and son-in-law Hay that in the coming presidential election, sentiment in the Southern states might swing in favor of another candidate.

Trade Policy

Regional differences emerged in the dispute over the imposition of protective tariffs, similar to those in the Missouri Compromise. While the Mid-Atlantic and New England states advocated a significant increase in the protective tariffs set in 1816, mainly against England, in order to protect domestic manufactures, the Southern states were strongly opposed. Since England was the most important market for their cotton, they ultimately feared for their economic existence if this trade relationship were severely impaired. In the speech delivered at his second Inauguration in 1821, Monroe avoided any determination on this question. The following year he advocated, in moderate terms, better protection for American manufactures. In the spring of 1824, the dispute intensified, with the coming presidential election campaign playing an important role.

1802

april 9. to Cap.ᵗⁿ austin
on acc.ᵗ of Major Hall
for the hire of slaves   114
p.ᵈ Mob.ᵗ Cowley
on acc.ᵗ of services   26.
being in full to this date
p.ᵈ M.ʳ Craig for hay   34.
the Sheriff of Henrico
for taxes   10
p.ᵈ Taylor o.M. for 1
barrel of sugar ——   25½
M.ʳ Forrester for beef 3½
⅃ p.ᵈ to Gardner & Mitch-
ell for M.ʳ Potter in Fred-
-burg to acc.ᵗ of my brother
Joseph ——   1000
p.ᵈ to De Forrest in full   12
1337 for 6.ᵗⁿ of coffee ——   1½
10. p.ᵈ to Col: Gamble
on acc.ᵗ of his Judgm.ᵗ
ag.ᵗ G. Webster in absequ.ᵗⁱᵉ   110⅓
in obedience to an order of
y.ʳ word of £ 50. in pa.ᵗⁱ

april
10. p.ᵈ for two saws for y.ᵗ 2½
p.ᵈ to Col: Carring-
ton in acc.ᵗ of Judge
Mercers estate ——   177.99⁄₁₀₀
p.ᵈ to M.ʳ Davis poin
ting in full for postage 9.
⅃ to acc.ᵗ of my private act. 3
p.ᵈ to M.ʳ Anderson
on acc.ᵗ of the Land
of Joseph my brother 2.00
p.ᵈ for chinsett.
wash bowls ——
⅃ some jugs ——   5.
p.ᵈ for 50. panes
of glass and 3 barrels
of Plaster of paris not
made by Gen.ᵉ Shee —— 49.
p.ᵈ M.ʳ Munson
full ——————   40

Economic crisis of 1819 and budgetary policy

At the end of his first term, the economic crisis of 1819 broke out. During this economic and financial crisis, exports collapsed, there were credit and bank defaults and a rapid decline in property values. As a result, cuts had to be made in the state budget in the following years, mainly affecting the defense budget, whose growth to over 35 % of the total budget in 1818 had in any case been observed with alarm by the conservative Republicans. Friction subsequently arose in the Cabinet when Secretary of the Treasury Crawford, who since his narrow defeat in the decisive caucus in the 1816 presidential election considered himself Monroe's natural successor, took the opportunity to make departmental cuts to his rival Calhoun. Joining the alliance of Crawford and conservative Republicans was Clay, who was primarily concerned with eliminating the network of military forts that Monroe and Calhoun had created in the Louisiana Territory. Clay, who was very close to this goal, saw private commercial interests threatened by the military posts. While Monroe's fortification program survived the cuts unscathed for the time being, the target size of the standing army was reduced from 12,656 to 6000 in May

1819. The next year, the president's pet project took a hit, and the budget for fort reinforcements and expansion was slashed by over 70%. Finally, by 1821, the defense budget had shrunk to $5 million, about half of what it had been in 1818. When the austerity measures went so far as to strip Jackson of his general rank, Monroe reacted with shame and appointed Jackson military governor of the Florida Territory.

Transport policy

Westward expansion and increasing domestic trade between the southern states, the Northeast, and the new states brought the construction of national transportation routes to the forefront, which was the focus of the first two years of Monroe's presidency. Policy discussions centered primarily on the issue of connecting the East Coast and the Ohio Valley west of the Alleghenies. In his last year in office, Madison had still vetoed a bill to finance the construction of such transportation routes with federal funds through the Second Bank of the United States because of constitutional concerns, and had previously called for the establishment of constitutional foundations through the passage of appropriate amendments. This view was opposed in particular by Clay, who was the principal advocate of the western states in Congress. Nonetheless, Monroe vetoed the decision by Congress to support improvements to the Erie Canal with federal funds. While he recognized the need for national transportation infrastructure projects, including with respect to military mobilization, he, like Madison, saw them as the responsibility of the individual states. Midway through his first term, Monroe successfully drafted a compromise formula in a veto message against the imposition of tolls on the National Road, which connected the Potomac and Ohio Rivers. Under it, Congress had no right to build interstate transportation routes or to manage them, but it could appropriate funds for them. The use of federal funds was subject to the requirement that they serve the common defense and welfare of the nation, not just that of a single state. Thereafter, Washington could fund infrastructure without interfering too deeply with individual states' rights.

Presidential election 1820

Monroe announced his candidacy for a second term early. At the Republican Caucus on April 8, 1820, the 40 members voted unanimously not to field an opposing candidate to Monroe. The Federalists did not field a presidential candidate of their own. Monroe's reelection therefore produced the clearest Electoral College result in American history behind Washington's unanimous election as president in 1789. Only one of the 232 electors, former New Hampshire Governor William Plumer, voted against him and for Secretary of State Adams, who did not run. Among the reasons given by Plumer was that he wanted to prevent Monroe from becoming president unopposed, like the great Washington. Even ex-President Adams, as leader of the Massachusetts electoral college, voted for his former bitter political opponent, Monroe. In addition to the lack of opposition, this uncontested victory by Monroe was rooted in his successful efforts to overcome orthodox Republican dogmas and thus further open up his party. This broad consensus did not survive Monroe's presidency, and by the next presidential election, personal disputes and conflicts between interest groups dominated events. These intraparty tensions replaced the antagonisms between Republicans and Federalists of the first party system that stemmed from differing philosophical views. Despite this broad approval in the presidential election, Monroe had few loyal supporters in the parallel-elected 17th United States Congress and correspondingly little influence.

Monroe Doctrine

In January 1821, in a conversation with British Ambassador Stratford Canning, 1st Viscount Stratford de Redcliffe, Adams first expressed the idea that the American double continent should be closed to further colonization by foreign powers. Whether Adams was the originator of this idea or others, including Monroe, came up with it independently at about the same time is not clear. According to Hart, the growing self-confidence of the United States that speaks from this guiding principle would have been difficult to imagine without the conclusion of the Adams-Onís Treaty. During negotiations on the Oregon Country frontier disputes, Adams expressed the principle to the British and Russian ambassadors in the summer of 1823 that the further settlement of America, with the exception of Canada, should be in the hands of the Americans themselves. The principle of "America to the Americans" quickly became a kind of theological creed in Monroe's administration.

After France, on behalf of the Holy Alliance, ended the Spanish Revolution of 1820 with victory at the Battle of Trocadero in August 1823, Secretary of War Calhoun and British Foreign Secretary George Canning, a cousin of Stratford Canning, warned Monroe that European powers might intend to intervene in South America. This increased pressure on him to comment on the future of the Western Hemisphere.

In August 1823, correspondence ensued between the British foreign secretary, the American ambassador in London, Richard Rush, and Adams, following up on his remarks about the decolonization of South America to Stratford Canning in January 1821. The purpose was to explore a common position regarding possible French intervention in South America, which Britain saw as threatening its commercial interests in that region. Canning had signaled that his country was willing to make a joint declaration opposing recolonization and to work with the Royal Navy to thwart possible attempts by the Holy Alliance to regain Spain's lost colonies in South America. When Monroe was presented with this correspondence, which had led to no concrete result, in mid-October 1823, his first impulse was to accept the British offer. Not wishing to pass lightly over George Washington's dictum not to become involved in foreign alliances, he sent the correspondence to Jefferson and Madison with a request for advice. In doing so, he suggested to his two predecessors in office that in the future any European interference in the affairs of South America should be considered a hostile act toward the United States. Jefferson responded that he welcomed joint action with Great Britain against European interference in South America, and he essentially summarized what later became known as the Monroe Doctrine. Madison also advised Monroe to accept London's offer. On October 23, 1823, Rush sent a message to Adams informing him of Canning's withdrawal from the voting process on a common South American policy.

Regardless of London's cancellation of a joint South American declaration, which probably did not reach Monroe until mid-November, the matter was discussed intensively and extensively in the Cabinet beginning on November 7, with Adams and Calhoun playing an active role in addition to the president. The occasion was the upcoming State of the Union Address, at which Monroe was to provide information on the state of foreign relations in addition to domestic issues. When Monroe asked Adams for a summary of U.S. foreign policy in preparation for the speech, Adams suggested a paragraph of principle. The wording was that in the future, with the exception of colonies that continued to exist, the independent American double continent should no longer be considered a colonizing territory of European powers.

By mid-November, the Cabinet was debating primarily the question of whether the positioning on South America should be unilateral or joint with Great Britain. After Monroe received Rush's message of October 23, he realized that London no longer considered Holy Alliance military intervention in South America likely. On November 21, he informed the Cabinet that he intended to present a doctrine concerning South America in the *State of the Union Address.* Monroe saw this matter as a unique opportunity to assert the strength and interests of the United States and to define itself as a nation. However, for the time being, the Monroe administration lacked the means to close the gap between rhetorical aspirations and actual influence in Latin America.

Monroe and his Cabinet eventually agreed to align the wording of the passage with two memoranda from the Secretary of State to the Russian and British ambassadors sent shortly before the State of the Union address. To avoid potential points of attack, the President deleted a paragraph by Adams that addressed the basic republican principles of the United States. The purpose of the dispatch to the Russian Embassy was to emphasize that the principal addressee of the Monroe Doctrine was the Holy Alliance. In this message, Adams made it clear that, except for Spain's military effort to restore its established colonial power in South America, the United States was not willing to accept the interference of any other additional European power.

On December 2, 1823, Monroe finally presented the revised contribution to foreign policy in his seventh State of the Union address. The principles, spread over three paragraphs, became known first as the *Principles of 1823* and later as the *Monroe Doctrine*, which, despite its importance, was never codified. Their first mention followed in a paragraph addressing negotiations with Russia over the Pacific Northwest, the next two in the context of historical relations between Europe and the United States. In all, six principles can be derived:

1. The American double continent is no longer an object for the acquisition of new colonies or recolonization by Europe.

2. Any European power that wants to extend its monarchical system to a territory in the Western Hemisphere is considered hostile.

3. Although the United States did not want to interfere with existing colonial relations between South America and Europe, it would regard any attempt by Europe to regain colonial power over the independent republics of South America as an unfriendly act.

4. Unless circumstances changed significantly, for example through Holy Alliance intervention, the United States would remain neutral in the war between Spain and its former colonies in South America.

5. The United States does not want to interfere in internal European affairs and expects the same from Europe in return.

6. European alliances, in this case the Holy Alliance, should not attempt to transfer their monarchical system to any part of the Western Hemisphere.

In particular, the fifth principle, which emphasizes reciprocity, illustrates that the conventional understanding of the Monroe Doctrine as a unilateralist declaration was not complete. Moreover, a subtext of the Monroe Doctrine was to allay European nations' fears of a missionary America that would militantly oppose colonialism and monarchy worldwide. According to Ammon, the doctrine had only a moral character for Monroe and no imperialist pretensions. He sees Monroe's humiliating diplomatic defeats in Europe as helping to shape the 1823 principles. Hart locates the central message of the Monroe Doctrine in the fact that it proclaimed not to tolerate or exercise hegemony, even though it later served as a justification for American imperialist claims to power. The most important consequence of the Monroe Doctrine remains that it established the Western Hemisphere as independent of European influence. In this interconnectedness of national security and foreign policy, Monroe went further than any previous president.

On the one hand, historians emphasize the decisive influence of Adams on the content of the doctrine, but on the other hand they point out that it was Monroe's decision not to confine it to confidential diplomatic notes, as Adams had wished, but to make it known worldwide through the State of the Union Address. Monroe himself was aware that he could not bind incoming presidents to the principles of 1823 with this declaration. Nevertheless, the Monroe Doctrine became the most impactful and widely discussed statement of foreign policy by any president, which Hart attributes to its logical structure. For many citizens, it has the status of gospel, although few know its specific content. While the Monroe Doctrine received much approval in France and Britain, Russia and Prince Metternich received it with disdain, viewing it as a revolutionary act without taking concrete hostile action against it.

Retired

On March 3, 1825, James Monroe passed on his office to Adams. Partly because of the heated political atmosphere at the end of his term, Monroe shied away from participating in political events. In retirement, oppressive money worries plagued him: as ambassador to Europe during the 1790s and 1800s, he had had to take out substantial private loans to fulfill representative duties and diplomatic protocol because of the mediocre pay. He had asked Congress for an allowance as early as 1797 and had waited in vain for payment ever since. Later, as minister under Madison and president, he had not pursued the matter, considering it improper in such a position. Even in the last days before handing over office to Adams, Monroe went through the personal papers of the previous three decades on the matter and wrote to Jefferson and Madison asking them to support him in his claims against Congress, if necessary. In 1826, Congress recognized part of the claims. Monroe, who felt he had been treated unfairly and had been forced to sell Highland to the Second Bank of the United States for lack of funds, was not satisfied with this and over the next few years tried to obtain from Washington a full appropriation of his expenses at the time. In Congress, he encountered resistance from the factions around Jackson, Crawford, and Calhoun, who resented him for earlier conflicts and accused him, among other things, of partisanship for Adams in the presidential election of 1824. It was not until shortly before his death, when he was living impoverished and dependent on private patrons in New York City, that he received a moderate payment in this matter, which was enough to pay off his creditors but not to restore his former standard of living. Further marring his final years was a resurgence of hatred and resentment against him as president over the Missouri Compromise and Jackson's invasion of Florida.

Contrary to original plans, Monroe did not spend his retirement in Highland, but for the first five years at his Oak Hill residence in Loudoun County. He had already resided there in the summer during his presidency. He filled the time with daily rides and experimented with new farming techniques to increase the harvest. In addition, he devoted himself to reading, his private library containing over 3,000 books, many of which he had acquired during his sojourns in Europe. Monroe was working on a work of political theory with the unwieldy title *The People the Souvereigns, Being a Comparison of the Government of the United States with those of the Republics Which Have Existed Before, with the Causes of their Decadence and Fall,* which, like an autobiography, remained unfinished. Like his two predecessors in office, he deliberately refrained from influencing the policies of his successors.

Having during the presidency discontinued his joint engagement with Jefferson and Madison at Central College, which became the University of Virginia, he now resumed a seat on the university's *Board of Visitors.* At the annual examinations in July, he presided on the Board of Examiners. When there was considerable indiscipline among the students, Monroe proposed in a report in 1830 the inclusion of military drill in the curriculum, but Madison refused.

Although already clearly marked by age and severely impaired in health by a riding accident in 1828, Monroe attended the *Virginia Convention* in Richmond beginning in October 1829. After western counties threatened to secede from the state, this convention was called to revise the Virginia Constitution. At the heart of the conflict between eastern and western Virginia was representation in the Virginia Congress and census voting rights tied to land ownership. The western counties wanted only whites considered in the drawing of voting districts for the Virginia General Assembly, since only 50,000 of the 750,000 slaves were in their territory. They also called for a relaxation of census voting laws because they favored eastern counties with their large plantations. The eastern planter aristocracy, on the other hand, feared for the future of slavery if western Virginia wielded too much political influence. Although Monroe favored compromise, thus putting him between all stools, he was elected as a delegate to the convention because of his high standing as ex-president in Loudon County. As elder statesmen, he presided over the Virginia *Convention* meeting at the *Virginia* State Capitol after Marshall and Madison cancelled. With Madison, he unsuccessfully proposed a compromise at the convention that provided for the Virginia House of Delegates the reform of representation demanded by the West, while in the Virginia Senate electoral districts continued to take into account the number of slaves in the assessment. Before the *Virginia Convention* ended, Monroe was forced to leave it for health reasons in early December 1829.

Shortly before his death, Monroe was hit by severe blows of fate in the family when his son-in-law and close advisor Hay died on September 21, 1830, and only two days later his wife Elizabeth. Hard hit, Monroe had to be taken into care thereafter and moved in with daughter Eliza Hay to live with his younger daughter Maria Hester in New York City. There, material hardship eventually became so great that he was forced to sell Oak Hill. On July 4, 1831, Independence Day, Monroe died in New York City.

Monroe was buried three days later in New York Marble Cemetery. President Jackson ordered a nationwide day of mourning. The public was moved by Monroe's death, not so much because of his accomplishments as president, but because with him one of the last prominent Founding Fathers had died. In response to an offer to that effect from the governor of New York, made about 1856, Virginia Governor Henry A. Wise and the Virginia General Assembly agreed to a transfer of Monroe's remains to his home state. He was interred in Richmond's Hollywood Cemetery in a cast-iron tomb completed in 1859. The governors of Virginia and New York were present at the ceremony and in their eulogies invoked the unity of the American Union.

Afterlife

Historical assessment and personality

A complete critical edition of Monroe's writings does not yet exist. Since 2003, Daniel Preston has been editing a collection of sources that is to comprise a total of ten volumes. The project is entitled *The Papers of James Monroe* and is based at the University of Mary Washington. Still considered the most balanced biography on Monroe is *James Monroe: The Quest for National Identity (1971)* by Harry Ammon. More recent works cited by Wellenreuther as relevant include *The Presidency of James Monroe (1996)* by Noble E. Cunningham and *James Monroe (2005)* by Gary Hart.

In traditional short biographies, Monroe is usually described as less dazzling and presumably intelligent than the other presidents of the Virginia dynasty, which consisted of Washington, Jefferson, and Madison in addition to him. To his credit in this conventional understanding of history, the Monroe Doctrine is emphasized, although Adams is considered its actual author. Hart, in his biography, comes to the conclusion that Monroe was a much stronger and independent personality than is generally believed. He had been, with the exception of Washington, the first president whose primary motive throughout his political career had been national security. Monroe's defense policy and the creation of a stringent foreign policy orientation by means of the 1823 Principles had laid the foundation for the United States' dominance of the American double continent and a more active role in world politics. He was the first president to view and define national security not only from an Atlantic perspective, but also from a Pacific one. According to Hart, Monroe does not rank among the great presidents, but his tenure was historically significant and as momentous as those of predecessors Jefferson and Madison.

Monroe owed success in what were actually competing goals of national security and expansion to diplomatic greats like Adams, less polarized domestic politics in the *Era of Good Feelings* at the end of the First Party System, and the Missouri Compromise. The Compromise allowed five new states to be admitted to the Union, so that by the end of Monroe's term it consisted of 25 states. The Missouri Compromise, which Monroe experienced as the greatest crisis of his tenure, only makeshiftly bridged the country's division over the slavery issue but held the American Union together for the next nearly 40 years.

Many historians and biographers point out that Monroe's interest in diplomacy and foreign affairs is better documented than that in defense and security policy.

According to Hart, this is because most of what is known about Monroe's administration comes from the records of Cabinet members, and those of Secretary of State Adams are more detailed and comprehensive than those of Secretary of War Calhoun. Monroe, he said, had been a hands-on president who had used his executive powers to the fullest, allowing Calhoun more latitude than Adams. After Monroe's presidency, the last of a veteran of the American War of Independence, it had become increasingly difficult to differentiate between foreign and national security policy.

Monroe was shaped politically by three important contemporaries: Washington, Jefferson, and Madison. Jefferson and Madison in particular, as immediate predecessors in office, cast a long shadow over Monroe's presidency. Less gifted and well-read as a rhetorician and political theorist than these two, he was nonetheless familiar to some degree with the classics because of his law classes with George Wythe. Reflective enough to recognize Madison's and Jefferson's magnitude of mind in comparison with his talent, he nevertheless did not allow himself to be side-tracked in the political business, but developed great ambition in his career in office. While the relationship with Washington was difficult and did not end well, Jefferson remained a lifelong friendly advisor and mentor to Monroe. With Madison he cultivated an equal political partnership, which at times was overshadowed by tensions without tarnishing their friendship. As an overall personality, Monroe was strongly influenced by his Virginian roots.

Like Washington and later Jackson, Monroe was shaped as a diplomat and politician by his military career. He therefore viewed the future of the young republic primarily from a defense and security perspective. He was a man of action with a leadership instinct, rather reserved and formal, in which he resembled Washington. Like the latter, he was more practically oriented than John Adams, Jefferson, and Benjamin Franklin, which is why he never reached their diplomatic stature. On the other hand, Monroe's strict division into a Western, republican hemisphere and an Eastern, monarchical hemisphere was easier to handle. While Jefferson anchored the republican ideal in the consciousness of Americans through speeches, Monroe made it the official state principle. As a pragmatist, he had a finer sense of current political trends than Jefferson and Madison. Nevertheless, unlike Jefferson, he did not actively seek to build a political following, but saw the politician as someone called to serve society without imposing himself.

Monroe placed the highest value on personal honor, dignity, and respect, which was also his most significant human weakness. When he was criticized or denied recognition, he saw it as a personal challenge that called into question the intellect, expertise, or sincerity of his character. In such cases, he did not succeed in simply passing over it, but had to defend himself compulsively, even if this meant endangering friendships and long-standing acquaintances.

Monroe was the first president to recognize the paradox in which the America of the Founding Fathers was trapped: the classical republicanism of the Greek polis, defended by citizen-soldiers, applied to a state structure many times larger. Taking their cue from Charles de Secondat, Baron de Montesquieu, they resolved this contradiction by creating a federation of republics. With expansion, this foundation was no longer tenable, so Monroe broke with this principle, even though he himself was a staunch and convinced party soldier. He created a new republicanism that put national security, guaranteed by a regular army, first. Monroe thus laid the groundwork for the large professionalized armed forces that characterized the 20th century. Hart sees Monroe's ability to adopt programmatic content from political opponents and thus create lasting broad majorities as exemplary for future presidents, such as Franklin D. Roosevelt. Nevertheless, Monroe was on the whole very strongly attached to classical republican ideals, which accounted for his deep distrust of the motives for action of John Adams and Hamilton, but also for his enthusiasm for the

French Revolution, in which he tended to see a continuation of the American Revolution.

Monroe's collaboration with Adams was extremely fruitful, making it difficult to separate the accomplishments of one from those of the other. According to Ammon, the cornerstone of Monroe's foreign policy was to give America the respect and recognition due an independent republic, and the key concept here was honor. His presidency is one of about a half-dozen that permanently defined America's self-image and role in the world. Wellenreuther sees the achievements in foreign policy as a major accomplishment of President Monroe. While Adams achieved their concrete implementation, the president created the necessary conditions for it.

Monroe's presidency was in an extraordinary period of transformation: the old order dominated by the Founding Fathers was disappearing, while at the same time America was trying to stabilize its relations with the European powers. Frontier disputes in North America were eliminated during this period, except for the British one in Canada. Domestically, Missouri's accession to the United States exacerbated the slavery issue at the same time that westward expansion intensified. Hart compares this development, which necessitated a more mature approach to security policy issues, to a teenager entering young adulthood. Monroe can be classified as belonging to the first phase of American presidents. At this time, incumbents were ideologically influenced by works from classical antiquity and the Renaissance, as well as English state theorists from the 17th and early 18th centuries, with the *Idea of a Patriot King* by Henry St. John, 1st Viscount Bolingbroke, having the most impact in particular. The concept of a "patriot king" ruling over self-reliant and virtuous landowners, alien to party strife and conflicting interests, held particular appeal for Southern planters and slaveholders, from whom the Virginia dynasty sprang. This traditional consciousness increasingly came into tension with progress, which manifested itself in commercial profit-seeking, individualism, and economic advancement. As presidents, Jefferson, Madison, and Monroe sought to exercise the office as apolitically as possible, even though they had previously been instrumental in the party dispute between Federalists and Republicans. Monroe seemed to have almost achieved her goal of ultimately making parties superfluous after the decline of the Federalists, but social reality caught up with this traditional thinking. Already under Monroe's successor, irreconcilable antagonisms broke out within the Republicans, which made President Adams a marginal political figure and led to his defeat by Jackson.

Honors and monuments

In 1824, the American Colonization Society named its settlement, founded two years earlier near Cape Mesurado, after Monroe, which became the capital of Liberia as Monrovia. Seventeen counties in the United States and Fort Monroe National Monument bear his name. Monroe Hall is dedicated to him on the University of Virginia campus. In Fredericksburg, Virginia, the house where Monroe operated a law practice from 1786 to 1790 has National Historic Landmark status as the James Monroe Law Office. The same is true of his burial site, the James Monroe Tomb, in Richmond and his estate home, Oak Hill. The Highland estate, located adjacent to Monticello and occupied by Monroe and his family on and off until 1830 between extended periods of absence, is listed as a monument on the National Register of Historic Places (NRHP). The remains of Monroe's birthplace are also listed on the NRHP as an archaeological site under the designation James Monroe Family Home Site.

The Presidential Dollars series, launched in 2007, minted coins in 2008 with the portraits of Monroe, Adams, Jackson and Martin Van Buren.

Movies

- *Life Portrait of James Monroe* on C-SPAN, April 12, 1999, 145 min. (documentary and discussion with Daniel Preston and John Pearce).

Other books by United Library

https://campsite.bio/unitedlibrary